"In this profound reflection on divine absence and presence, Charles Bartow presses his life-long passion for a Christian theology of sound toward a faith-filled theology of sight—written with tender, tensive care for those who 'have not seen and yet believe' (John 20:29). These poetic gems revel in the ordinary details of a tree bent in the wind and a rabbit escaping the talon. They ache to be read aloud, or in the case of his hymn texts, sung with hopeful defiance. Bartow's friends will recognize his characteristic joy, in spite of storm and doubt and loss. In a season when so much frays the good, he tells the truth he sees: 'Christ Jesus bends to meet earth's need.'"

—Jerusha Matsen Neal, Associate Professor of Homiletics, Duke University

"Charles Bartow's collection of 'late life' poetry speaks like a daily devotional. As spoken word, his work offers a window into the God of Scripture, the God of creation, and the God of his very own soul. In their brevity, the reader will be tempted to read many at a time. Perhaps one a day is better to savor the poet's grace-filled view of the world."

—David A. Davis, Senior Pastor, Nassau Presbyterian Church, Princeton, New Jersey

"Charles Bartow, ever the teacher-preacher and ever the word-smith, offers us a feast in this new collection of poetry. Poetry, Bartow writes, is 'best understood as blood turned into ink.' Here readers will find profound contemplations drawn from both the Bible and the natural world. There is much real blood-become-ink here, but not without play, whimsy, and delight—in short, a 'beauteous iconography'—and lexicography!—of grace."

—Brent A. Strawn, D. Moody Smith Distinguished Professor of Old Testament, Duke University

"As technologists promise our humanity can be surpassed, Charles Bartow's wry and faithful poetry revels in 'the human prospect,' exchanging artificiality for delight in the 'undigitized' real, to the praise of a God who did not surpass our humanity, but gladly embraced it."

—Matthew J. Milliner, Professor of Art History, Wheaton College

God's Beauteous Iconography of Grace

God's Beauteous Iconography of Grace

Poems Drawn from Scripture and the Book of Nature

CHARLES L. BARTOW

RESOURCE *Publications* · Eugene, Oregon

GOD'S BEAUTEOUS ICONOGRAPHY OF GRACE
Poems Drawn from Scripture and the Book of Nature

Resource Publications
An Imprint of Wipf and Stock Publishers
199 W. 8th Ave., Suite 3
Eugene, OR 97401

www.wipfandstock.com

PAPERBACK ISBN: 979-8-3852-6467-4
HARDCOVER ISBN: 979-8-3852-6468-1
EBOOK ISBN: 979-8-3852-6469-8

VERSION NUMBER 04/02/26

For my grandsons:

Alexander, Victorio, Miguel, and Mateo,

And

My parishioners, students, teachers, and colleagues ever patient, challenging, and encouraging across the years.

AS HAS BEEN SAID

God Himself is the best Poet,
And the Real is his song.
Sing his truth out fair and full,
And secure his beautiful!

Elizabeth Barrett Browning, 1844

Note: See Browning, "The Dead Pan," in Scudder, *Complete Poetical Works*, 191.

Contents

As Has Been Said | vi
Artistic Reflections | xi
Note of Invitation | xiii
A Word of Gratitude | xv
Alone I Hear You Speak | xvi

I

A Prayer for Illumination | 3
Advent 2022: The Human Prospect | 4
Commencement Address | 6
What Can Be Said of Mediocrity | 8
Form Becoming Thought | 9
Christ's Soul at Prayer | 10
Winter's Peace and God's Peace | 11
By Divine Right | 12
A Wave Goodbye | 13
What Ought to Be | 14
The Beginning and the End: A Summons | 15
Our Tenant Maxine's Happy Plant | 16
Naming the Holy Wholly-Other | 17
Late Spring Blossoming | 19

II

What Advent Means for Me, for You? | 23
A Modest Victory | 25
Let God Be God! | 26
If Only Trees Could Speak | 29
Color Me Joy | 30
Count Me Out! | 31
The Face of Love | 33
Red Fox Racing | 35
Invitation to a Walk | 37
In Depression Thoughts of Love | 39
Coffee with Calvin | 40
The Trooping World of Nature | 43
Springtime Winterscape | 45
Horrendous Evils and the Flame of Love | 46

III

An Advent Cry: AD 2024 | 51
The Elm Leaf's Seven-Colored Life | 52
The Wooded Path with Spring-Fed Stream | 53
Taking Turns? For the Birds! | 54
Humperdink | 56
Hymn: AD 2024 | 58
What Role to Play? | 59
What's at Stake in Prayer? | 60
Hear Nature Sing! | 61
We Two One | 62
Deus Absconditus | 63
Monet's Wish | 64
Papa, Mama, Goldfinch, Gone | 65
Wondering—Waiting | 66

IV

Come Little Children | 69
Early Morning Chitchat | 70
Everlasting, Everliving Hope | 72
Weathering Storms | 74
The Chance | 75
A Not Quite Silent Sound | 76
Early Cold Morning Musings | 77
Inside Out | 78
Easter Memory | 79
All May Be Well | 80
Hats Off! | 81
October Song | 82
Christmas Eve Psalms | 83
A Last Try | 84

V

Christmastide Troubling | 87
Family Hard Times' Fun with Uncle Lou | 88
Skyscraper Aspirations Met | 89
The Cup of Forced Solitude | 90
The Test | 91
Morning's Quiet, Calm, Welcoming | 92
December Spring Song | 93
Life: Hell Bound? | 94
In Memoriam | 95
Nightmare | 96
A Belated Celebration of Nature's Blessings | 98
When I Was Poor in Spirit | 99
Comportment Under Stress | 100
The Future Ill Housed? | 101

VI

Sad Christmastide Comfort | 105
Word, Sacrament, Prayer | 106
The Reach | 108
Is It Not a Wonder | 110
The Poinsettia, Crocuses, the Communion of Saints | 111
Falling in Despair, a Breath of Life | 112
Not of a Feather Together | 113
Daily Bread with a View | 114
A Subject Caressed | 115
A Prayer of Lamentation | 116
Let's Cup Ourselves a Lightning Bug | 118
The Pretender | 119
Narcissus, Daffodils, Cynthia Rose | 120
Our Beginnings Know Our Ends | 121
After All | 123

Off the Bookshelf | 127

Artistic Reflections

A Prayer for Illumination | 2
The Trooping World of Nature | 22
The Wooded Path with Spring-Fed Stream | 50
Inside Out | 68
In Memoriam | 86
Not of a Feather Together | 104

Note of Invitation

Your interest in my little book of late-life poems excites me. I hope your reading of these poems proves worth the effort. That would encourage me to believe my composing of them worth the effort.

Informed by a Christian devotional reading of the scriptural hymnody of ancient Israel, my poetic efforts seek to find and follow the path of godly wisdom, offer praise to God, and cry out to God in grief, confession, and confusion. As is the case with all biblical poetry, thought concerning the flourishing of human nature is inextricably bound up with the flourishing of God's entire created order.

Poems, I am convinced, are best understood as blood turned into ink. The purpose of reading them—especially out loud—is to turn the ink back into blood. The life of a poem is realized in the embodied speaking of the poem.

Thank you again for your interest. And thank you for your presence and your voice which I hope you will lend to my poet's ear, and eye, and sense of smell, and taste and touch. Great thanks to you for your life-giving self.

Faithfully yours,
Charles L. Bartow

A Word of Gratitude

My gratitude is owed to so many, I hardly know where to begin or end. The number of scholars, friends, and colleagues who have cheered me on with their knowledge and wisdom cannot be tallied. To them all I say thank you from the bottom of my heart.

My bookshelves are lined with the works of "my betters" as I call them. Their contributions are in biblical studies, speech and preaching, dogmatics, and practical theology. As must be clear, my vocation is the ministry of word and sacraments. I seek to be a servant of the Word and a servant of the servants of the Word. My betters in my avocational interests also have stocked my shelves: poetry, the oral performance of poetry, and music (especially vocal music).

My daughters, Paula Sue Suarez-Hevia and Rebecca Jane Bartow, true mentors of the art of teaching, have made important critical contributions to my thinking and writing. Paula Sue also typed the text of this volume for the publisher. My eldest daughter, Emma Marshall, honored for her work in foster care and adoption and civic life in Fairfax County, Virginia, when young, accompanied my wife and me on many tours of duty in preaching and in the performance of poetry and song. As she used to say as we got into the car to set out: "Buckle up for danger!" My next-to-eldest grandson, Victorio Charles Suarez-Hevia (Tori), provided the artwork for this book of verse. His talent is an inspiration.

Above all, always, thanks to my wife, Ruth Paula Goetschius Bartow. She has cared for me with great skill and patience and measureless affection for nearly sixty-two years. She typed my master's thesis, my PhD dissertation, and my first book, *The Preaching Moment: A Guide to Sermon Delivery*. In my first book of poetry, *Dust and Prayers: Poems* (Cascade), I offered this tribute:

ALONE I HEAR YOU SPEAK

For Paula

The wood is solitude of sound and sight,
And here the ear can listen, just as light
Can cut a shaft through limbs and leaves to grass
To tinge bright gold the quiet green I pass.
Alone, I hear you speak in every blade;
Your voice the glistening hush upon the glade.

I

A Prayer for Illumination

A PRAYER FOR ILLUMINATION

1 Kgs 19:12; Ps 19:1–4; Isa 40:8; Matt 11:15; 2 Tim 3:16

The texts of Scripture, silent as the light
Of vanished stars still gleaming through the night,
Forever speak, if we could only hear
Their silent sound of Holy Spirit fear
That Awful Presence overwhelming sense
With beauty far beyond the eloquence
Of human vocal, verbal gesturing,
Such beauty as makes barren deserts sing.
God, train our ears to hear, our eyes to trace
Your beauteous iconography of grace.

ADVENT 2022: THE HUMAN PROSPECT

A POST-EMERSONIAN PERSPECTIVE

For Roger, *être humain*, d. Sunday, November 20, 2022

No "Over-Soul" for me, I long for God,
Not human vaunt writ large, fancied belief
That human beings, living souls reveal,
Time to time, a fully human prospect:
Transcendent Human Being, now perceived
By the discerning eye of mature minds,
Enlightened minds, set free from creedal thought,
The self-revealing God of Holy Writ,
God's means of grace: Word, sacrament, and prayer.
It's human being of itself re-formed,
A force of nature, not of nature's God.
No! I wait, incarnate, very God
And in that, the humanity of God
True fully human prospect stable-housed
Among the meek inheriting the earth
The beauty of the Infinite disclosed,
Wrapped in swaddling clothes, God's garb of glory.

Note: For background, see these elegantly composed essays of Ralph Waldo Emerson (1803–82). Emerson's essays (here critically considered as a challenge to traditional Christian thought) seem to me still to influence, or to find resonance in, a good deal of contemporary, secular, and ecclesial thought: "Man the Reformer" (1841), "Worship" (1860), "Self-Reliance" (1841), and "The Over-Soul" (1841). Emerson, *Essays and English Traits*, 43–85, 133–48, 275–95.

In the poem above, reference is made to two important twentieth- and twenty-first-century theological writings: Barth, *Humanity of God*, and Hart, *The Beauty of the Infinite*. See also the Gospel According to Matthew 5:5.

COMMENCEMENT ADDRESS

GETS A COVERT, PUZZLED RESPONSE

"Live your truth," the youths were told,
"Be yourself, authentic, bold.
Make the world a better place,
Shape the future of the race,
Each and every one of you
Saying, doing what is true,
What is right in your own sight,
Go for it with all your might!"

One young grad thought otherwise:
"Foolishness!" was her surmise,
"Hubris to believe it true
Keeping one's own self in view
Is the future of the race,
Leave behind, without a trace
Thought of one way, truth, and life?
Plural truths, somehow end strife?

Hail, the Princess of the peace
Mirrored in myself! Wars cease
With my truth, others with theirs
Celebrated, unawares,
Unconcerned there just might be
Truth beyond plurality?"
This, the graduate felt sure
Left truth's future quite obscure.

Obscurantism must hide
What the present can't abide.
All felt sensibilities
Lauded, honored verities,
That's the truth the present age
Revels in, considers sage.
Yet the present too must pass
Yielded to new selves. Alas!

In such selves, the future's spent
Every hope and dream outlent,
Given in a moment's time
To a present thought sublime:
Present selves full, free, and fair,
Beautiful beyond compare.
Grasping all of truth, thought wealth:
The illimitable self.

WHAT CAN BE SAID OF MEDIOCRITY

Not quite up the daunting slope to midpoint,
He stopped awhile to rest and look back down
To where he'd started on his upward trek
To reach the highest height he could attain,
If not the summit—the peak next to it?
The obstacles he faced along the way,
Each hour, each day, each year stirred up a fear
He'd never make it far as he might hope,
His progress, hard, discouragingly slow.
Just why he struggled up this Everest
When life afforded him easier climbs
Less steep, less hazarded by obstacles
To test, to mock his strength, his skill, his heart,
One cannot guess. But climb he did despite
The inner scorn he felt, the heartache sore.
The heartache stopped for good a short way past
Where he had stopped before to rest, look back.
His life achievement: mediocrity.
I'm not a Latin scholar, but I know,
I looked it up, and mediocrity
Means halfway up the rugged mountain slope.
I wouldn't mind myself to climb so high.

FORM BECOMING THOUGHT

Wait, wait for form, Frost said. Form waits for me
To find the words well suited to express
Those acts, and thoughts and feelings form allows.
Some things cannot be said in sonnet's scheme,
In rhyming couplets, even in blank verse.
Free verse is roomier, but then it too
May be too limited in size and shape
To house just anything that one might say.
But that's the gift of form. Form constrains thought,
Insists upon what only can be said
This way or that. Form sets me on a search
To find the just-right words and order them
To say what's on my mind, yet suits the form.
Form liberates the mind's emerging thought.

Note: See Frost, "Pertinax," in Latham, *Poetry of Robert Frost*, 308.
See Ammons, "Corson's Inlet," in *Collected Poems 1951–1971*, 147–51.

CHRIST'S SOUL AT PRAYER

Heb 7:25, KJV

I'm led to think our Blessed Savior's soul
At prayer is like the birch that bends in storms
But never breaks. It rights itself again
Still trailing leafy branches to the ground
Like tears of love once and forever shed.
Just so Christ Jesus bends to meet earth's need,
Our Great High Priest at prayer, world without end.

WINTER'S PEACE AND GOD'S PEACE

Phil 4:7

The winter lives outside my window charm,
The hemlock, pine, and fir, the Norway Spruce,
Its groaning limbs, snow-covered, swooping down
To kiss the hard earth's face with sweetest care.
These towers of winter green are welcoming,
Hospitable to chipmunks and to squirrels,
And to my shy yet bold red cardinals,
My black-capped chickadees, juncos as well.
It's life, the great and small of it at peace,
Creation's wintry heralding of God's peace
And yearning, groaning for that peace God-sent,
Our souls groan, yearn for, scarcely finding words,
Such peace surpassing all understanding.

BY DIVINE RIGHT

"...[All persons] are endowed by their Creator with certain unalienable Rights.... Among these are Life, Liberty and the Pursuit of Happiness..."

The Declaration of Independence

Also Luke 10:7

By some regarded as of no account
Who swept the floors, dusted the furniture,
Washed the linens and clothes and made the beds
And cleaned the bathroom sink, the toilet bowl,
She thought herself entitled to respect:
"Good morning ma'am," and "Thank you very much,"
A living wage, as though the laborer
Were worthy of her hire, to cite a phrase.
Such dignities, she thought, were hers by right:
Life, Liberty, Pursuit of Happiness,
Each, all, endowment of the living God
For her, for everyone the whole world round.
Most would say—who would not?—she got it straight,
Her life a witness to a gift divine.

A WAVE GOODBYE

"The world is too much with us," Wordsworth said.
May still be true for some, but not for me.
The world's passing me by, I can't keep up.
Technologies outpace my competence
To think, to feel, to work as once I did
When I was young and schooled in media.
What media there are these days speed up
The flow of information crowds now crave
To think, to stay in touch, to feel alive.
This world's no passing show, but old men are,
And I'm among the old men stumbling through
What time's left us to wave the world goodbye.

Note: Wordsworth, "The World Is Too Much with Us," in *English Poetry*, 674.

WHAT OUGHT TO BE

"To be or not to *be*, that is the question." Wm. Shakespeare, *Hamlet*.

What's been written once was said,

And what was said was done.

Fact and deed perceived then led

To speech, the three made one.

It is sense gave rise to thought,

Felt sensing of the mind.

Is—what is—issued in ought.

Imperatives we find

When indicatives are sought.

Note: Italics in the line from Shakespeare's *Hamlet* quoted above indicates emphasis as the line was performed by Sir Lawrence Olivier. Shakespeare, *Tragedy of Hamlet, Prince of Demark* 3.1.56.

THE BEGINNING AND THE END: A SUMMONS

Rev 21:5

Just recently heard this report,
That miles beneath the crust of Mars,
Red Planet waters, vast and deep,
Hold promise life may yet be found
Where all seems waste and ruin, death.
Good news! Perhaps a parable
The Book of Nature holds for us,
Reflecting what the ancient text
Of Holy Scripture boldly tells,
How, in the end, where death seems sure,
Fresh promised life is brought about.
Then let us now hear this glad word:
The Alpha and Omega speaks,
"See, I am making all things new."

OUR TENANT MAXINE'S HAPPY PLANT

Her "happy plant" we call it,
the thriving Christmas cactus
close by Maxine's kitchen door
budding in August no less.

Can't pass it without a smile.
It makes glad, lifts our spirits
as if the season's at hand
in which such cactuses bloom.

But December's months away,
its rousing "Joy to the World,"
its family fun and feasts
and its fireside caroling.

Just the same, we will take it,
this out of season budding.
After all, can't Christmas joy
be welcomed the whole year round?

Bud on, bud on "happy plant!"
Make every day Christmas day!
Even in sad, troubling times
paint on our faces a grin.

NAMING THE HOLY WHOLLY-OTHER

Gen 1:1; 1 John 4:8

In Scripture God is distant from what's made,
Is Holy, Wholly-Otherness apart.
The cosmic wonders wrought and being wrought,
The beautiful and terrifying worlds
That have been, are yet, and are yet to be,
Incomprehensible in scope, beyond
What human thought can dream up or control,
Seemingly inhospitable to life
As known on planet Earth, which life itself
Is full of threats, many as promises.
These cosmic wonders lead to wondering
Just who this God may be whose handiwork
Is so much more than words can ever tell.
Shall human beings think of God as All
Or think of God as SCOPE, THE ULTIMATE,
The "Ground of Being" if being's grounded?
BIG BANG appears to be NOTHING disguised,
A whimpered cypher, human thought's full stop.
Well, back to Scripture then to see what's there.
And there we find it said that God is LOVE,
That life on earth, elsewhere, is dear to God
Whose Holy, Wholly-Otherness is love.
Poetic sense echoed that scripture word
A full, long seven centuries ago.

Dante Alighieri spoke of God's love
"That moves the sun in Heaven and all the stars."

Note: Alighieri, *Paradiso* 333.129. For "the ground of being" see Tillich, *Systematic Theology* 1.112, 116–17, 140, 147, 155–58, 205, 209, 235, 238, 244, 246, 284.

LATE SPRING BLOSSOMING

Magnolia blossoms flourish in the warmth
Of late spring's welcoming bold, colored life,
The deep, rich purple beauty that so charms
The artist. I watch her as she sets up
Her easel, canvas, and lays out her paints,
Her watercolor tablets, unfolds her
Canvas chair, sits down, takes hold her blond-stemmed
Dark-haired, thin-pointed brush. She holds it still:
Precisely how to start? I understand
That watercolor painting takes great care.
Mess up at first, there is no going back.
Her artist's skill's practiced dexterity.
Her quick, alert brown eyes, her brunette crown,
Her clear cream-colored skin, strong, shapely limbs
Draw my attention, not so much away
From the magnolia as to how to frame
Within a photograph magnolia charm,
Human allure, a single rare beauty,
A late spring blossoming, capture, hold it
Warm, vivid in memory years to come.

II

The Trooping World of Nature

WHAT ADVENT MEANS FOR ME, FOR YOU?

Jer 8:22

It's Advent and what's coming gives me pause.
What's coming's not just Christmas, Bethlehem,
The babe in swaddling clothes, the manger scene,
The virgin Mary who birthed Jesus there
With Joseph standing watch stalwart in love.
It's not just shepherds hearing in night skies
Heavenly anthems, peace on earth, good will.
No, with all that, the meaning of it all,
God's Word, made flesh, his holy law fulfilled,
No slightest letter of it unobserved;
Arrival of God's Son, true light from light
Makes clear what's been concealed in the dark,
Secreted contradictions of God's will
Revealed. Advent's "good news"? God's judgement day.

My self-inflicted wounds of sin are healed,
Not lightly but with penetrating balm,
The stinging, burning Balm of Gilead
The prophet sought to heal his people's wounds.
Christ Jesus is God's healing judgment come,
His birth, his life, his suffering, his death
At sinners' hands, his being raised is grace,
For me, if you'll allow, trial by fire,
A burning up of my defiling thoughts,
My lawless ways, my pride, self-righteousness,
Pretended virtues all gone up in smoke.

And in this loss that's gain, felt burning salve,
I do not think I'm by myself alone.
Christ's Advent gives me pause. But what say you?

A MODEST VICTORY

Rom 12:3

Perhaps like me you've felt depressed at times,
not clinically sick at heart perhaps
but just "bummed out" as the expression goes,
in the pursuit of happiness dead last.

Take heart, dear friend, it seems we're not alone,
instead we've got great company, a world,
a universe of melancholic souls.

But that can be depressing in itself,
to find you're not exceptional at all
but pretty much like everybody else.

It could be then, the best thing we can do
is lighten up a bit, laugh at ourselves.
The bromide is, "Laughter's good medicine."
Let's have a dose and give ourselves a break.

If platitudes don't work, we'll laugh them off,
that way we'll have a win to celebrate:
a modest victory, but it will do.

LET GOD BE GOD!

A Sermon on Temptation in Verse

Matt 4:1–11; 1 Cor 1:23b; Deut 6:4

It is written, so it's thought, in what we know
of earth, of skies, of seas, of planets, suns.
It is written in the farthest galaxies,
in light-years' distant realms, cosmic events.

In living things we may discern it written,
in fields, and forests, creatures large and small.
It is written in the busy lives of cells
such microscopic wonders as amaze.

It is written clearly in the human mind
that we're to take the measure of it all.
It is written we shall conquer worlds unknown,
lay claim to, make good use of what we find.

All accounts of evolution state this fact:
the arc of our hegemony's set there,
our genetic heritage our destiny.
It is written the human species rules.

It is written in our ancient, sacred texts,
human beings, fashioned in God's image,
are granted vast dominion in God's name.
The whole of His creation's in our charge.

Yet danger is inscribed in what is written,
a clear and present danger Scripture notes,
temptation to adamic overreaching,
our grasping what belongs to God alone:

Wisdom, and power, and glory, and honor
such as makes of us gods unto ourselves.
This zenith of our self-regard's demonic.
The devil mouths our challenging of God

He tempts God's Son, the Christ, the second Adam
with cunning use of hypotheticals.
"If you're the Son of God"—it begs the question—
"turn stones to bread." Now there's a trick we'd cheer!

"It is written," so the Christ, God-sent, replies,
it's written, "no one lives by bread alone."
What is needed's Spirit food for famished souls.
If God's our God, we'll feast upon His Word.

Yet the tempter, like God's Christ, can quote God's word,
his lie God's truth applied to godless ends.
"It is written he will command his angels
concerning you and . . . they will bear you up . . ."

In other words, if Christ so choose, he could plunge
into our grasping life with angel hosts,
legions of angels to see that he's crowned king,
all opposition cowed, no cross, no grave,

No history of outrage, crucifixion
and frenzied talk of resurrection hope.
"Christ crucified," should we call that Christ's gospel?
It's strange "good news," defies all common sense.

Human "real-politic" now on his mind,
the demon-tempter gives it one more try.
All kingdoms, principalities, and powers
he'll give God's Christ if Christ declare him Lord.

Christ's rebuke comes certain, swift: "Be gone! Be gone!
for it is written . . . 'Worship God alone . . .
and serve only him.'" When all is said and done
we're not, as thought, the center of it all?

It is written that the center of it all
is God Himself. We, made in God's image,
are to bear his image humbly, prayerfully
and only so exercise dominion.

In the earth, the skies, the seas, and distant realms
among God's living creatures large and small,
we are to serve as stewards of creation,
not self-appointed masters of it all.

Reading, heeding what is written we shall cry:
Christ is victorious, let God be God!

IF ONLY TREES COULD SPEAK

Gen 1:31

If only trees could somehow speak to me,
Might what they speak be music to my ears:
Their spreading roots in pianissimo,
Their sap flowing steady tempo largo,
Their leaves, wind-blown, the reeds of clarinets,
Their flailing limbs a storm-thrilled timpani,
Their life entire a symphony of love
Composed, conducted by a loving God
Who, listening more eagerly than I
Calls everything he hears, oh! very good,
His opus in the cadences of praise?
If only trees could somehow speak to me,
Might what they speak be music to my ears?
Might what I hear stir praise within my heart?

COLOR ME JOY

The fog this morning, high, non-threatening,
Holds subtle shades of gray I cannot count.
Somewhere above the fog of course there's sun
And many shades of blue, white scudding clouds.
It pleases me to note this while I sit
Here drinking coffee, black, no sugar, cream.
It's clear as day the black's not ebony,
But more a dark brown, melancholic tone,
Brown study's what it's called in verse and prose,
Though, tell the truth, right now I'm feeling fine,
No blues, no browns, no foggy grays, pale whites,
But rather cloudless skies of sunny joy.

COUNT ME OUT!

The digitally well-connected crowd
Considers me an oddity, I'm told.
I'll grant that, as they see things, I am odd.
I never learned to type. I cannot text,
Create a Facebook page, check out smart phones.
Consider me not bright enough for that.
Got almost left behind in middle school,
Not up to snuff, you might say, downright odd.
Now that was long ago and far away
But I can't say that things have changed a lot.

Our present age, post-human, scholars say,
Is all "AI." Well you can count me out,
No artificial anything for me.
I'll settle for the real anytime.
Now it's been shown the real's pretty slow
And prone to countless flesh-and-blood mistakes,
Mistakes, if you don't mind, I'll settle for.
These flesh-and-blood miscues are honest wrongs,
No slightest artificiality.
"AI's" so perfect it's praised as unreal.
Beyond these noted grand profundities,
Let this old odd-ball make a final point:
The disconnected, solitary world,
Undigitized, is such a pleasant place

As lets me—old, mistake-prone oddity—
Think, say, do, live precisely as I please,
No matter the connected crowd may scold
And urge me to get with it for a change.
Let the crowd count me out; I could care less.
Well that's my case. It no doubt has its flaws.
But be that as it may, it's really mine.

THE FACE OF LOVE

1 Cor 13:7

Sometimes the face of love's tear-stained;
Its lines speak sadness, grief, and loss
Etched in by time and circumstance,
Acidic personal regrets,
The breaking off of friendship's ties.
The style of envy cuts its grooves,
Its sharp, hard point an instrument
Of almost unmatched skill, sure craft;
The master craftsman, one's own self.

And yet, across the face of love
A wrinkled beauty may appear,
Deep lines of wisdom gained through years
Of hardship suffered, wrongs brought on,
Inflicting pain, body and soul.
Still, somehow, inner strength was found
To smile and not give up, endure
What had to be endured with grace
That outlasts time and circumstance.

With you and me, what will it be?
We can't be certain, do not know
The future. It's not ours to write
What time and circumstance obscure
With all that happens in the now

To quicken happiness or grief
Or both at once in memory.
I knew a woman, twinkle-eyed,
Came through it all face lined with love.

RED FOX RACING

Five-thirty a.m. a red fox
racing across my yard,
his magnificent tail
a bushy train of glory.

Catches and keeps my attention
catch, keep anybody's.
Was he chasing breakfast
before I'd eaten my own?

Was he instead being chased
and running for his life,
as is said, running scared?
My guess: chasing his breakfast.

He's gone, time for me to get mine,
my breakfast that is, eggs
or maybe cereal;
frosted wheat bites will do.

After my breakfast shall I run,
so to speak, for my life,
to escape it, find it,
chase down what's left of it?

That would be no magnificent
    race with train of glory
        trailing across the yard
            of years that are left to me,

Just some wearied human pursuit
    catching no attention,
        colorful as wheat bites.
            Think I'll have my coffee now.

INVITATION TO A WALK

Sirach 30:15 (An Apocryphal/Deuterocanonical Book)
aka Ecclesiasticus

Well here we are
    at our kitchen table.
Had our orange juice
    and our doughnuts and prunes.
We're good to go.
    Shall we venture a walk
around the block?
    We're not up to much more
of course, too old.

    Kind of chilly out there,
we'll bundle up,
    grab our rolators, go.
What do you say?
    Why the hesitation?
The sun is out,
    come on, we can do it.
Cold air's bracing,
    just keep moving along.

Bet our neighbors
    will be greatly impressed.
"Those old duffers,"
    they'll say, "can't keep them down."

Their praise of us,
    nothing better than that.
Celebrities
    of a sort; so we are.
Put on your coat.

     I'll put my coat on too.

Let's get going.
    No good sitting around.
The kids tell us
    we should walk every day,
keep up our strength,
    and see what's going on.
Never can tell
    what we'll find around the block.

IN DEPRESSION THOUGHTS OF LOVE

Lam 3:19–24

Depression is the inner enemy
That turns the mind's eye from what it might see
Outside the present moment's dark despair,
The light, the gladness, joy that waits out there
Beyond the inward darkness and the gloom
That comes of thinking all there is, is doom.
But if the eye is lifted up above
Its present inward gaze by thoughts of love,
Depression can't maintain its dreadful sway,
Instead its hold is loosed, night turns to day.
Love's inextinguishable light reveals
The goodness, living hope depression steals.

COFFEE WITH CALVIN

Divine Election and the Resurrection

1 Cor 15:53; Col 3:3–4

Been reading in the *Institutes*
Each morn from five o'clock to nine
Much more than I can understand:
Divine election unto life
For those deserving no such thing,
But rather death, the second death,
The fate of those thought reprobate
And banished from the company
Of gathered saints enjoying God
Eternally, eternally,
Now clothed in sanctifying grace,
Baptized, that is to say, in Christ,
Attired in incarnate love
God sent to salvage human life
From all that would despoil it
Eternally, eternally.

Another awesome mystery:
The resurrection of the flesh,
Quite foreign to Platonic thought,
Absurd to Manichaean sense
Wherein the flesh despised, more, feared
Is jettisoned that souls may soar

To heaven's heights magnificent
And filled with spirit presences
Untrammelled by earth's crying needs,
Eternally, eternally.

But earth, with its inhabitants
More than restored, is beautiful
In holiness, the holiness
Of holy love incarnate in
Our vulnerable flesh, God's Christ
Reviled, pierced through with hate, contempt,
Cursed, hung upon a tree to die.
Yet see his palm pierced hands, his side,
Christ's wounded, healing flesh alive
Eternally, eternally.

In him alone we live and move
And have our being, you and I,
Companions of the saints in light,
All sainted sinners glorified,
Our life at last revealed God blest
Eternally, eternally.

Note: On the matter of predestination (to salvation or eternal ruin) see, e.g., the *Institutes*, 984 and following. Calvin warns against pretension to excessive clarity regarding the subject for the matter has to do with God's "secret judgment" which is beyond the reach of human exploration. Calvin's thought on predestination is grounded in Scripture and follows a trajectory of interpretation set by Augustine. In a word, salvation is by grace alone and not in any measure inclusive of human merit.

As regards the resurrection of the flesh see, e.g., pp. 998–99 of the *Institutes*. Calvin cites 1 Cor 15:3 regarding the corruptible putting on incorruption and the mortal putting on immortality. He draws on Tertullian and, again, Augustine in dismissal of the Manichaean opinion that the flesh is inherently and irredeemably evil, a creation of the devil and not of God. To sum up: life in Christ is manifest in mortal flesh, and matter matters.

THE TROOPING WORLD OF NATURE

Gen 1:24–25

How glad I am the world of nature troops
Each day its varied fauna through our yard,
Red foxes, happy rabbits, hungry deer,
Box turtles, chipmunks, squirrels, all the while
The keen-eyed red-tailed hawks soar high above.

Our avian feeder welcomes such a range
Of brightly colored visitors who sing
Their happy northeast songbird tunes as set
Our aging hearts to beating singing joy.
Were you here with us you'd be singing too.

There are, of course, from time to time events
Of tragic consequence: the raptor's prey
Swept up to soundless death, the road-killed fawn,
Clear evidence of pain and suffering
Endured time and again, no letting up.

No wonder our aged hearts beat their lament:
"This should not be!" And yet, and yet it is.
A curse it seems to us, a dreadful wrong.
But nature's terror's happenstance, not plot,
The handiwork of predatory minds.

That cruelty's a strictly human trait.
We have our homicides, our genocides,
Our fratricides, infanticides, and more.
In nature there is death, not faunicide,
No dealing death for profit or for hate.

Let's leave the matter there and turn on back
To where our blank verse musing had its start,
The world of nature trooping through our yard.
Its varied species still invite a song
To satisfy our hearts—and minds—for now.

SPRINGTIME WINTERSCAPE

The Wisdom of Solomon 13:3c

The scene outdoor's a snowless winterscape;
The birdbath, filled, all ice, a skating pond
If only birds could skate. The sky is clear,
Is sunny, bright, but wintry cold north winds
Set tree limbs flailing, bark chips flying past
Whoever happens by this ice-cold scene.
Expected April showers late last night
Mean there's a chance for greening of the lawn
Whenever comes a late spring warming up.
The forecast for tonight is yet more cold
Sub-freezing temperatures, blankets of frost.
This winterscape is an anomaly
For sure, also a brilliant work of art.

HORRENDOUS EVILS AND THE FLAME OF LOVE

Matt 27:33–44; Mark 15:22–24; Luke 23:33–34;
John 19:16–18; Heb 12:28–29

To say that I am daunted
　　is to understate the fact.
Worlds of horrendous evils
　　surround me, they're all about,
Overwhelm me from within,
　　and frighten me, bring on scenes
That appall: an earth on fire
　　pole to pole with burning hate,
Roaring furnaces of hell,
　　and in my heart, secreted
There, more fuel to feed the flames.
　　I falter, I cannot cope
With what is, what's coming on.
　　I try to cry out, "Help God!"
But I choke on the ashes
　　of incinerated lives.

God's name, I'm told, means holy
　　fire to burn away malice,
Envy, ruinous desire.
　　Recall that sometimes burning
Dung heap hill named Golgotha;
　　three crosses there, on the one

God's own sacrifice of love
    Spirit fueled eternally,
Horrendous evils consumed
    By fire, reduced to ashes,
And, from out the ashes, life!

III

The Wooded Path with Spring-Fed Stream

AN ADVENT CRY: AD 2024

Matt 8:23–27; Mark 9:24; Ps 13:1; 46:10

Wild dogs of war still barking! Lord, how long?
Malicious ranting everywhere abounds.
Shall stormy seas all hope in God soon drown?

Lord Jesus, Son of God, we need to hear—
Above war's growling hounds, hate's crashing waves—
Your voice, your silencing rebuke: "Be still!"

As once you calmed the Sea of Galilee,
Freed fear-gripped souls, revived near-failing hope,
Now hear our cry: Come save us from despair!

Lord we believe: Help! Help our unbelief!

THE ELM LEAF'S SEVEN-COLORED LIFE

For Darian

How photographed I can't begin to tell
But there it is for anyone to see,
A single elm leaf's seven-colored life
From photosynthesized chlorophyll green
To rusty yellow, orange, crimson red.
The range of colors captivates me most,
Such beauty, such vitality as stuns
Me, turns my thoughts to wonder and to praise.
I multiply this stunning moment's art
By thousands, millions, tens of millions more
Across millennia of elm tree life,
And all this glory fraction of a whole
Artistic marvel none can dream, or tell,
Or photograph, or measure, comprehend.

THE WOODED PATH WITH SPRING-FED STREAM

John 4:14

Once upon a wooded path we strolled,
Sunny, but the wood provided shade,
Gave our walk a cool refreshing feel,
Breezes hot beyond the wood shut out.
Thought we'd take a break beside a stream
Gently flowing from a hidden spring
High above the path we strolled along.
Said you loved me, I said I loved you.
Still our love is strong, is mutual
Shade for us and shelter from life's storms,
Hot storms, fierce winds, wild imaginings;
Once pledged love prevents their breaking through.
Love's the wooded path we stroll today,
Freshened by a gently flowing stream.
High hidden spring its source, constant, pure.

TAKING TURNS? FOR THE BIRDS!

Matt 6:26a

By himself at the feeder
the tiniest of sparrows
happily plucking at seed
in our four-inch hanging dish.
The larger birds, the pigeons,
the mourning doves, the blue jays
the red belly woodpeckers,
mama, papa, cardinal
Not yet on the scene, but near,
will be taking over soon,
not scaring off the sparrow.
It's more like taking turns
As is their right, there being
little room for all the birds
to peck their meals at once.
Taking turns, that's the order
Of the day and all week long.
On the whole it seems to me
birds take turns better than we,
brought up to know that we should.
Don't always do what we should.
Sometimes we muscle our way
up to the front of the line
as if first place is our right

Our motto *carpe diem*
like any would-be Caesar.
"God helps those who help themselves,"
we say. Help ourselves a lot.

HUMPERDINK

A bit cute to be sure
    we named him Humperdink,
    the little wild bunny
    in his camouflage fur.
Nibbling through the clover
    and what passes for grass
    in our, without a doubt,
    laughably labeled lawn.
Unhurried, contented,
    so it seems, he nibbles
    and then hippity-hops
    along his merry way,
First to the locust tree,
    then to the magnolia
    and the fragrant lilac.
    Never minds me at all.
For I keep my distance
    since he's in no way tame.
    So he seems right at home
    short yards from our back porch.
From our bird feeder he's
    just a few feet away.
    Again, he's right at home.
    Don't be fooled, there's danger,

Certainly not from me.
    It's from that red-tailed hawk
    aka rabbit hawk,
    keen-eyed, circling above,
Hungry, eager for prey.
    But turns out rabbits run,
    hide, quick as a flash when
    sensing soaring danger:
A hawk's lightning descent,
    talons at the ready.
    No grasping a meal
    this time. Humperdink's safe.
Still, I'm disquieted.
    For little Humperdink
    there may yet come a day
    when his rabbit speed fails,
And his camouflage fades,
    he's got no help at hand,
    and his safe hiding place
    is just too far away.

HYMN: AD 2024

Tune: Toulon (Genevan Psaltar, 1551)

To God whose love sustains us all our days,
Let voices strong or weary render praise.
In joy, in sorrow God is always there
With tender mercy holding us in prayer.

In Jesus, God's dear Son, we find release
From conscience-stricken guilt. He is our peace.
He is the light of life who every day
Directs our steps along the homeward way.

From God the Father and from God the Son
The Holy Spirit comes to make us one
In heart and soul with Christ in God's embrace
Until at last in heav'n we take our place.

WHAT ROLE TO PLAY?

How long it's been this way I cannot say,
But seems to me it's been quite long enough.
Each day is like a decade's worth of gruff,
Dismissive threatenings, nothing to stay
The hand of powers hellbent, set to play
The part of gods, other lives but the stuff
Of dreams, shadows of dreams, mere dust and fluff
To be swept up or sneezed out of the way.
Call it the deep ambition of the soul
Writ large, self-assertiveness at the heart
Of the unconquerable self, of late
So prized. Yet still there is another role
To play soul-sized, the humbling costly art
Of love, God-sent, forever up-to-date.

WHAT'S AT STAKE IN PRAYER?

1 Thess 5:17

There is a need to pray today;
Well every day we need to pray,
But this day's prayers have urgency,
Especial urgency. You see
I have this feeling something's wrong,
That where there should be heartfelt song,
Fortissimos of grateful praise
In all the living of our days,
The human voice is giving out,
Finds little to be glad about;
Is dwelling sadly more and more
On frightful rumors, fears that war
Is on the way. Fear's not absurd
When so much of what's taught and heard
Is surely not good news. If true
That war's at hand, more than a few
Good reasons can be found to pray,
To pray today and every day
With urgency, sincere desire,
All souls aflame with Spirit fire.
It's life and death at stake in prayer;
It's kindled faith or else despair.

HEAR NATURE SING!

Ps 47:6, 7; Rom 1:20; Luke 19:40

Hear nature ever singing praise to God
With joyous ringing whale songs out at sea,
Finch peeping softly in a nearby tree,
An aspen. All its tongue-like leaves sing, laud
The hand that crafted them. They spread abroad
On gentle breezes nature's melody,
Worship that soars: "Holy, Holy, Holy!
Lord God Almighty!" Does their worship prod
Humanity to lend its voice in praise
Just as blest nature's praises ever sound
In seas, in soils, in "creatures great and small"?
If we keep silent, silent rocks will raise
Their hallelujah! Hear it now resound
To stir praise songs in you and me, in all!

Notes: "Holy, Holy, Holy! Lord God Almighty!" Reginald Heber, 1827, in *Glory to God*, hymn no. 1.

The phrase "creatures great and small" is from "All Things Bright and Beautiful," Cecil Frances Alexander, 1848, in *Glory to God*, hymn no. 20.

WE TWO ONE

Mark 10:6

Today's our anniversary,
The sixtieth for you and me.
The two of us, a long time one,
Will lift a toast in rhyme for fun.
And God grant us another year,
We'll toast ourselves, again and cheer
The passing of the years gone by
With hope for more years drawing nigh.

DEUS ABSCONDITUS

Ps 42–43; Ps 22

Unanswerable questions haunt my sleep,
Stirred up by taunting ghosts of disbelief.
"Where is your God?" they ask, but could care less,
I feel God's absence when I crave it most.
It's nothing new, this taunting disbelief.
The Hebrew poets wrote of it with tears,
Laments that still have resonance for me.
Responding to such taunts, the psalmist cried:
"I shall again praise him, my help, my God."
God's absence, thought embarrassment to faith,
Stirs up my hope and zeal for him. It makes
His absence seem his presence near as breath
To shout a loud, "Hosanna! Lord God save!"
The ghosts of taunting disbelief remain
But now are tamed to serve my troubled faith,
Keep it alert, poised, eager to proclaim:
    Praise God from whom all blessings flow;
    Praise him all creatures here below;
    Praise him above ye heavenly host;
    Praise Father, Son, and Holy Ghost.
        Amen.

Note: "Praise God from Whom All Blessings Flow," Thomas Ken, 1695, 1709, in Jones, *Hymnbook*, hymn no. 544.

MONET'S WISH

Matt 6:26a

Just yesterday I learned the great Monet
Wished he could paint the way a bird can sing.
I've not a clue precisely what he meant.
Was it the wild, free singing charmed him most,
The bird's flinging its notes into the air
While heedless of how they might be received?
Or was it the sheer spontaneity,
The winsomeness of nature's careless joy?
No matter. What amazes me the most
Is that he sought—this genius of a man
Whose works are celebrated through the years—
He sought to emulate untutored grace,
A bird, by instinct, bursting into song.

PAPA, MAMA, GOLDFINCH, GONE

The purple finch that visits now and then
Provides remembrance how things were back when
Bright goldfinch papa, mama came to eat
Some thistleseed, their staple birdfood treat.
They perched upon a lilac limb, their gold
And olive colors gemlike, truth be told
More stunning than the purple finch whose kind
Appearance, royal garb, brings them to mind.
I wonder why the goldfinches are gone.
It cannot be, when all is said and done,
They're gone for good. I sure wish they'd come back.
Our thistleseed is fresh right off the rack
It's stacked on at the birdfood store nearby.
Our lilac misses them; I hear it sigh
Whenever there's a breeze. Can't help but think
Some cunning neighbor's tempted them with drink,
A birdbath filled with goldfinch nectar, draft
Elixir, mixed drink of alchemic craft,
Addictive. Absurd conjuring you say?
Agreed. But why then are they gone away?

WONDERING—WAITING

Ps 14:1

It's fools say in their hearts there is no God.
That's written in the Bible, still it's odd
That though I do believe in God, I'm left
To wonder where my God may be, bereft
Of certainty that he is near. And yet
I will not act the godless fool, but set
My where's-God wondering to work. I'll strive,
Uncertainly, to keep my faith alive,
Expectant, for God may draw near to me
Through uncertain belief. I'll wait and see.
Or could it be that waiting's where God is
Already; set to let me know I'm his,
His waiting patient, eager, loving, dear?
With every breath I take God draws me near?

IV

Inside Out

COME LITTLE CHILDREN

Come little children, cherub choirs
Sing Christmas joy, light yuletide fires
Of faith, hope, love in hearts grown cold
From wintry hates and wars foretold
By Scripture's promised Prince of Peace
Who, in the end, makes wars to cease.
Into this present war-wracked year
Sing an angelic, "Do not fear."
Sing the host of heaven anthem
Heard in night skies near Bethlehem.
Sing "peace on earth, good will," sing awe
To all who find in manger straw
God's Christ child, Lord of heav'n and earth,
Of time as well, of grief and mirth.
Sweet cherub choirs come quickly, bring
Heartwarming news grown souls may sing.

EARLY MORNING CHITCHAT

Most mornings, very early,
I sit alone at the kitchen table
with my cup of hot chocolate,
and there I read
and think and write.
Some mornings, I think and write
well enough to believe
my morning's not wasted, but
profitable, other times
it's wasted time and ink.
As for my reading, that too
may be a morning well spent,
time with the Brownings,
Elizabeth Bishop, Langston Hughes,
for heaven's sake, Holy Scripture.
On other mornings, reading's
time wasted on news unnewsworthy
and certainly not new;
same old, same old commentary
on the passing scene:
The so-called really big show
of politics, the whatever
party playbill—left, right
middle, middle right, middle left.
Remember Ed Sullivan's "Really Big Show"?

So this morning, early,
alone, I scribble for you my
kitchen table chitchat,
my cup of hot chocolate
as I think and write.

EVERLASTING, EVERLIVING HOPE

The Native American Heritage and *e pluribus unum*

A Chastened Aspiration in Song

Forested regions, green and beautiful,
Were theirs, as were tracts of wilderness,
Broad fertile plains, rock-bound and sand-strewn coasts,
Two crashing seas, their sparkling inlets, bays.
Brooks, ponds, lakes, rivers, cool refreshing springs,
Prized hunting grounds, tilled fields of corn and grain,
High rugged mountain climbs, broad rolling hills
With fertile valleys, hamlets in between,
All we have made our own at first was theirs,
Still is, our land their homeland and their love.
Famed poet, prophet G. K. Chesterton
Titled them *The Everlasting People*
Who have in fact outlasted long, hard years
Of broken treaties, genocidal rage,
Then, too, and not of little consequence,
Uncherished contributions to the lore
Of a yet emerging complex culture
Resilient, welcoming and strong and free.
They've been displaced, replaced; they still go on
Seeking one day to find their way to hearts
Like yours and mine, rended, prepared to hear
At last the muffled tympany of praise
Within the still unfinished symphony
Of nature, Spirit—breathed into the lungs

Of humankind. The music makes it clear
We're theirs just as the land is theirs—and ours.
Hearts rent may sing *epluribus unum*
In everlasting, everliving hope.

Note: See Milliner, *Everlasting People.*

WEATHERING STORMS

Last night the sky pink hued, this morning red,
A sign perhaps that there's a storm ahead.
It's March, it's blustery, strong north winds blow
And there's a good chance they could bring in snow.
March is a most uncertain time of year
When what's up with the weather is not clear.
At times it's balmy, springlike, warm, and bright,
At other times it's wintry, snowy white.
If there's a storm a-coming, let it rain,
Not snow. Cold, slashing rainstorms might be gain,
A heralding that spring is on the way
And winter gone for good. I'd shout, "Hooray!"
Don't mind at all March storms that bring in spring,
But one more wintry blast's another thing.

THE CHANCE

Those persons, prominent, respectable
Of reputation indestructible,
In presence strong and bold, beyond all doubt
Forces of nature, so to speak, about
Them and their well-earned prominence, power,
What shall we say, do, who cannot tower
Above the crowd as certainly they do
But must scramble to gather up a few
Crumbs of accomplishment quickly forgot,
No sooner gleaned than tossed out on the spot?
Thus daunted, overawed by our betters,
Shall we make their successes our fetters
Binding us to felt mediocrity,
Or, inspired, chance "to be, or not to be?"

Note: "To be, or not to be: That is the question . . ." From Shakespeare, *Tragedy of Hamlet, Prince of Denmark* 3.1.56.

A NOT QUITE SILENT SOUND

Rom 8:26

At night, in bed, a not quite silent sound,
The faintest whimpering, as if the ground
Beneath the house, the town, the cosmic whole
Were trembling, groaning like some human soul
In travail, waiting, longing for release
From trauma, unnamed, destined to increase
For who can tell how long? How shall I pray
Tonight? Can't even guess what I should say.
That whimpering I hear, near silent plea,
That groan, will it go on eternally?
Is it a prayer, sad cry, its source unknown,
Ineffable hope, a deep yearning moan?
Whence the near silent sound I hear in bed?
Up from the ground? Down toward the ground instead?

EARLY COLD MORNING MUSINGS

It is early, Wednesday morning,
    very early; dark and cold out.
I am inside having breakfast,
    some orange juice, hot cream of wheat.
Have a vest on though the heat's up,
    mercury reads seventy plus.
Inside my skin I am dark, cold,
    dark in thought, ice cold in feeling.
All the world outside is freezing;
    inside my skin shall I soon freeze?
Some might tell me it's just old age
    got the better of me, that's all.
Well the "got the better of me"
    certainly is true enough. Yes,
I am bested, more than bested
    by the ravages of time, but
"That's all?" Well then let me tell them
    That "that's all" is more than I need
Of the dark and cold to make me
    think a lasting freeze may soon come
No vest and no hot cream of wheat
    has the slightest chance of easing.

INSIDE OUT

The old man notes it's spring outside,
Though inside—in himself—it's fall,
Late fall in fact. Soon winter comes,
Life's pulse slows down. It's downright cold
All through his aging flesh and bone.
His thoughts are shivering regrets,
A wintry mix of sleet, rain, snow.
Sleet coats his miscued memories.
A dreary rain of anxious thought
And whiteout snows bring loss of sight
Of all that's happening out where
Spring's budding, colorful and bold.
Yet still his old mind's eye can glimpse
Enough to make him realize
That shut up in his cold, old self
He's missing out on something grand.
So he decides it's not too late
To take once more the risky step
From inside fall to outside spring.

EASTER MEMORY

1 Cor 1:18–25

The little girls in cheery spring pastels,
The little boys dressed up like little men,
Proud, smiling parents, all of this that tells
Of Easter happiness parades into
The church of memory and brings a smile.
Here resurrection joy fills every pew.
Up front the pastor cries, "Christ is risen!"
All present shout, "He is Risen indeed!"
Glad they are to have this glimpse of heaven.
Into this happy scene, too soon recalled,
A troubling memory: Dramatic pause,
Pregnant with fears of strife, would have forestalled
This recollected joy, taint it with fact
Sharp-pointed, hard as nails driven through flesh
To wood: Christ crucified, a God-willed act
Of sacrifice incomprehensible,
Good Friday, Holy Saturday good news,
An Easter cruciform, nonsensical
Except to faith God-given; loss, grief, sin
Faced head-on, defeated; *this* Christ is *Lord*,
In Easter memory, death, life adored.

ALL MAY BE WELL

It's six o'clock a.m. and dark outside,
But in the northwest corner of the sky
The moon is full, big, bright, and welcoming
As if the night were trying one last time
To keep me in its warm embrace and care,
Away from all the troubles of the day:
Disheveled, anxious thoughts, neglect of prayer,
My discontent with old age, failing health,
My tottering around the house, the yard
Downhearted half the time, sometimes alert
To what the day might promise otherwise
Than such pathetic, grumpy self-concern.
The sky is brightening. Soon dawn will break,
The moon will disappear. All may be well.

HATS OFF!

My hat's off to the black-capped chickadee
Whose pecking at his dish of mixed birdseed
As I approach to replenish suet
And fill the tube-feeder with wild finch food.
I greet him in my chickadee-dee voice.
He greets me, eye to eye, no slightest fear,
And so I fancy him my black-capped friend.
Once I've completed what I came to do
And turn to leave, the chickadee takes flight
Alighting on a nearby Norway spruce.
While he's perched there I take my perch inside.
We have enjoyed each other's company,
The feasting, friendly chickadee and I.
So hats off to my black-capped feathered friend!

OCTOBER SONG

Ps 30:5b

October's morning air is chill,
The outside world is peaceful, still.
I find the stillness welcoming
Of old-time music I might sing
Oh, sometime later in the day
When up-and-at-'em, fast at play,
The neighbor children will not hear
My singing songs of yesteryear,
Glad-hearted tunes that are for me
A treasure-trove of memory.
Once had my own young playtime fun,
Fun to recall when life's near done.
Don't get me wrong, I'll stay around
Long as I can, enjoy the sound
Of quiet mornings yet to be
Filled up with lilting melody.
Don't know, don't have the slightest clue
What other aging folk may do.
But as for me, I say it's fine
To raise October's auld lang syne.

CHRISTMAS EVE PSALMS

1 Kgs 19:12; Luke 2:14; Rev 2:28

Lamentation

This Christmas Eve is dumb, no angels sing;
All heaven's quiet as a tomb tonight.
It is a Christmas Eve of darkness, fright,
A mournful eve wherein sad souls must fling
Their wearied hopes into a failing spring
Of love, of kindness, goodness. Oh! The sight
Brings an alarm. Shall wrong prevail, not right?

Praise

A still small voice, a sound of sheer silence;
  above earth's din, for those with ears to hear,
    the heav'nly host cries out, "Glory to God!"
      and herald angels sing of peace on earth,
        while, in the east, the *morning star* appears
          brightening westward through the deep of night.
            Amidst uncomprehending darkness—light!

A LAST TRY

The aging poet sits,
    and scowls at the blank sheet
        before him on his desk,

Surrounded by betters
    much older than himself,
        many of them long gone,

Decades, centuries gone.
    Their works remain, preserved
        in shelves on shelves of books

That mock his wordless scowl,
    the blank sheet on his desk,
        his failing thoughts—unversed.

In Memoriam

CHRISTMASTIDE TROUBLING

Luke 2:11–12

Is there a sight more troubling than this child
Newborn and tender, fair and meek and mild,
Who, grown up, will cast demons from the soul
And face down money-changers on the dole
Bled from God-fearing poor and desolate
Berated folk, short-lived and desperate,
Who ever throng the templed courts of pow'r
Hoping there'll be for them a God-blest hour?
The question stirs my wond'ring if for me
The troubling child, full grown, will always be
A blessed Presence to sustain my hope
Amidst the demon-dark through which I grope
Toward holy promised templed courts above,
Beyond all dolesome gain, spacious as love.

FAMILY HARD TIMES FUN WITH UNCLE LOU

Think back with me to all the fun we had
When times were tough, when things were going bad
To worse: No money in the till, the world
At war a second time, and young lives hurled
Into the theaters of conflict wild
With bayoneted dreams and hopes all piled
In heaps. Our grandma almost lost a son,
Our Uncle Lou, a soldier who'd poke fun
At you and me, most anyone around;
A happy-and-go-lucky sort who found
A game to play—he'd make them up—when back
From war on leave. Made us forget the rack
And ruin of our lives, provide a few
Good laughs to ease the stress. Thanks Uncle Lou!

SKYSCRAPER ASPIRATIONS MET

Matt 5:3; Luke 6:20

"Thou hast made us for Thyself, and our heart is restless until it repose in Thee!" St. Augustine

Skyscraper-high aspirations are found
With underpinnings, granite-like, more sound
Than is Manhattan's granite empire pride.
In city-dwellers' hearts high hopes reside
Well grounded in that human yearning blest
To human souls by God, yearning for rest
And unimagined peace, proffered, made known
In Jesus Christ, God's Son, in him alone
Whose Spirit-Presence fills Manhattan's streets.
Among the poorest of the poor he greets
The rich in things—but poor in spirit—throngs.
To all who yearn for rest in God belongs
God's Heav'n-sent Presence, peace. All souls are dear
Who, restless, seeking God, find him drawn near.

Note: Augustine, *Confessions*, 11.

THE CUP OF FORCED SOLITUDE

Ps 25:16

Time and circumstance could soon silence me,
But I'll keep listening long as I can.
At least for the time being that's my plan.
I say "for the time being," for you see
It is not clear just what the case may be.
I've auditory losses and they fan
An inward flame of anxious thought the span
Of my attentiveness will shrink. My plea
Is that that's not the case. You understand
How disquieting it would be to lose
Touch, contact, comprehension of what's up
In the world outside myself—all the grand
And dismal goings on. Who'd ever choose
To quaff forced solitude's deep, bitter cup?

THE TEST

Deut 6:16; 2 Cor 13:5b

The wind was mezzo forte from the north;
It blew a strong allegro down the lane.
I struggled to stay upright. It was plain
I should have stayed inside, not ventured forth
Braving the elements, raw nature wroth
To have me prove myself against it, strain
To stay erect. A wobbly old man gain
The upper hand against such odds? What froth,
What outright bluster, vanity to chance
A trek along a windblown lane—snow, ice
Besides! "Foolish old man," I cried, "Help, God!"
I paused and gave myself an inward glance.
I wondered: could my prayer just prayed suffice
For ballast as, tested, the lane I trod?

MORNING'S QUIET, CALM, WELCOMING

This morning's quiet, calm and welcoming
And so I step with care into the day
Not wanting to disturb its blessed peace.
As best I can I keep at bay such thoughts
As bring disquietude: remembered slights
Received or, worse yet, given, afflictions
Of body, mind, and spirit. Peaceful times
Of quiet may be spoiled by unchecked hurts
That well up inside out, feelings of shame
For having failed to gain the upper hand
Controlling fear of failure in pursuit
Of happiness, not for myself alone,
But everyone for whom I have some care.
Each has a right to mornings quiet, calm,
Welcoming as is this peace-blest morning
That I step into carefully today.

DECEMBER SPRING SONG

December's brought an early chill.
I'm shivering, this should not be.
Can't help but wonder if it will
Go on this way. It's wait and see.
It's wait and see and hope as well
There'll be some warming up before
A record's set, a lasting spell
Of wintry cold. The outlook's dour.
"Hold on," I tell myself, "till spring,
A late spring thaw the end of May."
O happy spring, your blossoming
I wait for, yearn for, day by day!
Bing sings his dream of Christmas white
In his full, rich, warm baritone.
I dream, I sing spring blooming bright
While still chilled clear through to the bone.

LIFE: HELL BOUND?

Can wrongs be recompensed by doing good,
Whatever good may be? Some answer no
And yet insist that wrongs be paid up for
In any case, since victims have a right
To hold accountable any and all
Who have done them harm or, by circumstance,
Have profited from wrongs unrecompensed.
If we consider such a line of thought
Valid, it would appear that human life's
Strife-bound, a vain pursuit of attempted
Rectification of what cannot be
Rectified, the victim ever at odds
With the designated rectifier,
And this goes on and on time and again,
A living hell, if it's thought hell exists.
Does hell exist? Are other people hell?
Or is a peopled hell sophistic speech,
Hyperbole of brimstone and the pit?

IN MEMORIAM

H. R. and Cynthia Lanchester, d. August/September 2024

Matt 5:4; Rom 8:38–39; Phil 1:21; 1 Pet 1:3; Rev 14:13; 20:12; 21:17

How many we have loved are dead and gone!
How blessed is the memory of each
Whose name is written in the book of life
Opened eternally unto our God!
Therefore we do not grieve as without hope;
Our hope's a living hope secured by God,
Creator and redeemer of us all,
The comforter of those who trust in him,
The joy of those for whom to live is Christ,
To die is gain, to know God's steadfast love,
The joy Christ Jesus knew in facing death:
God's promised resurrection of the dead
As is attested in God's written word
And witnessed in our facing death—and life!

NIGHTMARE

Epistolary Fiction

Dear Sigmund,
The nightmare that came on last night,
The strangest one I ever had,
Still haunts me now I'm wide awake.
I'm writing you, my dear young friend,
So you can give me your advice,
What it may mean, what I can do
To rid myself of its effects:
Depressing thoughts like thoughts of death,
How brief, how meaningless life is,
Or so it seems much of the time.
What do you think, should I go on,
Think this thing through unto the end
Whatever that turns out to be?

I was asleep yet felt awake,
Knew I was lying flat in bed,
When suddenly I felt strong arms,
Much stronger than mere human arms,
Reach round me from behind and squeeze.
Thought sure my ribs would crack, my chest
Collapse, my lungs give out. Can't breathe!
I thought for certain I would die.
I grabbed the arms around me, yanked.
To no avail, or so it seemed,

When suddenly the squeezing stopped,
Then just as suddenly resumed.
I screamed your name, or tried to scream.
Surprising, since you weren't around,
You came, said gently, "What is wrong?"
I woke and realized I'd dreamt
A nightmare dream of consequence,
And dreadful, unforgettable.

I'm writing you to ask what I
Should do, if anything, to rid
Myself of this weird nightmare scene
That simply will not go away.
Or will it disappear in time?
I know my physiology,
Have pioneered psychology.
Of this, young friend, you are aware.
But dreams of consequence are your
Domain. If you've a chance please write
And let me know what's going on,
What this dream means, what I should do.
Till then, sweet dreams. Your nightmare friend,
Wundt

Note: Wilhelm Max Wundt, 1832–1920, physiologist-psychologist. Sigmund Freud, 1856–1939, the father of psychoanalysis. Wundt was German, Freud, Austrian. Wundt was considered the father of modern experimental psychology. I've no idea, but doubt Wundt and Freud knew each other well if at all. This letter in verse is fiction start to finish.

A BELATED CELEBRATION OF NATURE'S BLESSINGS

Ps 16:6a

As vowed I'm trying here to sing a song
Of gratitude for nature's blessings long
Enjoyed, but left as yet to celebrate.
The hour has come. I hope it's not too late,
I'm growing old. A hummingbird takes flight.
Dawn lights the dew-damp vanishing of night.
The pungent sweetness of the lilacs fills
The air, and nearby woodland music thrills
My waking heart with melodies: the peep,
Peep, peep of cardinals, the graceful leap
From tune to tune of mockingbirds. Light breeze
Comes up and gently swirls black locust leaves,
Floats pink-white locust blossoms to the ground,
Hushed pianissimo of snowflake sound
For those with hearing more acute than mine
That's failed of late, young ears close to divine
Perhaps? Well, be that as it may, let me
Say this: soft snowflake fall's a memory
Heard clear as day, and if you will allow
Its memory helps me fulfill my vow
To honor nature's gifts to me as best
I can. Belated gratitude expressed,
My stricken conscience finally at peace,
My celebrative singing I will cease.

WHEN I WAS POOR IN SPIRIT

(This hymn may be sung to the tune: Morecambe)

Matt 5:3

When I was poor in spirit, near despair,
The Lord my God in mercy heard my prayer.
All through the darkness of encircling night,
His Spirit guided me with love's pure light.

God gave me courage, strength to face my fears,
In tender mercy wiped away my tears.
Wherefore my glad thanskgivings I will sing
And unto God my grateful tribute bring.

O God, your love sustains me day by day.
You sent your only Son to be the way,
The truth, the life my yearning soul must trace
Till welcomed in your Fatherly embrace.

O gracious Father, Son, and Holy Ghost,
The choirs of heaven, all high heaven's host,
In sacred anthems bless and laud your name.
Let me, with them, your majesty proclaim.

COMPORTMENT UNDER STRESS

Ps 1:6

How to comport oneself in times of stress?
The question can't be handled with finesse
For time itself is stressful, takes its toll,
Time and again diminishing the whole
Of what's been thought right, good, and happy, true,
And worthy of respect, keeping in view
A wide range of opinion on that score.
But who'd opine we should not all abhor
Relentless time's diminishment of all
We human beings strive for to stand tall,
Content with having tried our best to live
With measured rectitude so as to give
Worthwhile accounting of ourselves, and say:
"Though stressed at times, we somehow found our way"?

THE FUTURE ILL HOUSED?

The Incarnation as Prolepsis of the Kingdom of God and the Consummation of All Things

Matt 6:10

Clear through the present, on into the past,
THE FUTURE finds in Bethlehem at last
Its starter home, a shabby, smelly stall
Within a neighborhood that would appall
The down-and-out street-dwelling poor—unknown—
Those hapless souls thought better left alone.
Imagine it: THE FUTURE there so housed!
Why not the slightest interest is aroused
Among the better off who'd make secure
A comfortable future with allure
All on their own, their having "come of age."
Let's face the fact such thinking's thought quite sage.
But is this lauded wisdom truly wise?
Or does THE FUTURE, scorned, spell its demise?

VI

Not of a Feather Together

SAD CHRISTMASTIDE COMFORT

We've such a Christmastide as has not been
Played out in our family life, not seen,
That is to say, for many years: ill health,
Few gatherings with feasting, but a wealth
Of disappointments with remembrances
Of once upon a time rich fragrances
Of evergreens, like incense in the air,
And happy season's greetings, party fare.
Then carols sung in praise of Jesus' birth,
Emmanuel, God with us here on earth,
Felt presence of the Lord in all of life,
Heavenly peace amidst earth's fears and strife.
This Christmastide such recollections dear
Bring comfort, blest assurance God is near.

WORD, SACRAMENT, PRAYER

AND THE KNOWLEDGE OF GOD

John 4:23–24

Of heaven as of God what shall I say
Except I cannot know, I cannot bring
To mind, or heart, or soul such majesty,
Such uncreated beauty as must fill
God's holy dwelling place, his spirit-life,
Their being his alone to keep or give?
But God has brought his heaven down to earth,
Has made our human life his very own
In Jesus Christ his Son that we might find
His goodness, steadfast love, his righteousness
Within the meanest circumstances we
Have brought upon ourselves, our common life.
God's heaven come to earth is personal,
Is clear and present, fit to meet our need
Of rectifying grace to mend our speech,
To heal the wounds of those who've suffered most
From mean, uncaring, unforgiving ways,
And reckless words thrust weapon-like as swords
Into the heart of so-called enemies
Who could be, would-be friends in Christ, God's love
Incarnate in word and sacrament and
Prayer, audible as mended human speech
And visible as human flesh and blood.

Scripture attests Christ is the bread of life,
The cup of suffering he had to drink,
Which cup we share at his command, the cup
Of our salvation: eat, drink, come to know
And worship God in spirit and in truth.
"God is spirit and those who worship him
Must worship [him] in spirit and in truth" (John 4:24).

THE REACH

1 Cor 2:9 (KJV)

It seems the human mind's been forged to reach
Beyond what can be grasped by intellect
And made accessible to measurement
And analytic study using tools
Invented by the ingenuity,
The cognitive developments that are
The hallmark of the human race, explored
By depth psychology, behavioral
Psychology as well, a history
Researched through explorations into myth
And analyzed empirically too.
These calculated reasonings, for cause,
Are prized as grand achievements of our age,
The age of science and technology
Triumphant over out-of-date restraints.
We're left then pondering whence the desire
To probe transcendent mysteries so vast
As to exceed what human minds can grasp
Since they are mysteries outside all space
And time, not light-years distant, farther yet
Outside the range infinity suggests,
Infinity itself a finite thought,
A calculation of the human mind
Expressing the known limit of its reach.
George Santayana noted long ago

"The soul's invincible surmise." But yet,
Still farther back, Augustine, famously,
Declared the human soul a restless soul,
Unresting till it find its rest in God.
Philosopher and theologian both,
With contemplative rigor, echo this:
The psalmist's eloquent, poetic cry:
    . . . my soul longs for you,
        O God.
    My soul thirsts for God,
        For the living God (Ps 42:1b–2a).
I find within my heart, and soul—and mind—
Peculiar resonance for Scripture's song
And for "the soul's invincible surmise,"
Its restless yearning till it rest in God.

Note: Santayana, "O World," in Untermeyer, *Concise Treasury of Great Poems*, 397.
Augustine, *Confessions*, 11.

IS IT NOT A WONDER

Is it not a wonder
　　how often times gone by
　　　　refuse to stay gone by
　　　　　　but turn up in the now,
Sometimes as welcomed guests,
　　sometimes invading thieves
　　　　who rob me of my peace
　　　　　　and quiet contentment?
I've had my better days,
　　and worse days, heaven knows,
　　　　show up. Uninvited
　　　　　　recollections bring joy,
Sometimes disquietude.
　　Wish it were up to me
　　　　which past moments come by.
　　　　　　That's not the way it is.
Past moments come to mind
　　indiscriminately,
　　　　memories I'm proud of
　　　　　　or chagrined to recall.
My aging mind retains its long-term memory.
　　The short-term's more a fog
　　　　of unrecorded facts
Of life: such goings on
　　as I'd call gain or loss.
　　　　How shall I call it now?
　　　　　　Right now I call it gain.

THE POINSETTIA, CROCUSES, THE COMMUNION OF SAINTS

Eighty-one days since last Christmas,
    the poinsettia showing red
        but slowly turning crimson rust;
Next week it's spring, March twentieth;
    The early blooming crocuses
        about to show pale purple heads
Above a slowly greening lawn,
    cold winter's brown and yellow gone
        until October, Halloween
Or All Saints' Day November first.
    Most of my sainted ones, deceased,
        await my entering their rest.

FALLING IN DESPAIR, A BREATH OF LIFE

I'm weighted with despair beyond my strength,
A falling leaf off a forsaken bough,
No hope of a soft landing, cushioned rest
Upon a tender lawn, green, manicured,
More likely I will land on rocky soil,
The hard realities of dying days:
Griefs, losses, ruined dreams, false promises
And failed attempts to think, and say, and do
At least some one small thing for sure worthwhile,
A job well done, providing self-respect.
I'm falling fast and faster toward the rocks.
Then suddenly an upward draft takes hold,
Hurls me around, lifts me toward heaven's heights.
I catch a deep and thrilling breath of life,
And so inspired, my back against the rocks
That, till that moment, seemed my destiny,
I look ahead and up instead of down
And fix my thoughts on possibilities
That prayer alone can reach, sublimities
Like soulful peace, God's respite from despair.

NOT OF A FEATHER TOGETHER

Note: "Birds of a feather flock together."
We worldly wise women and men say that.
But at my bird feeder it's *au contraire*
the cardinals and goldfinches, sparrows,
the downy and red-bellied woodpeckers,
less frequently Baltimore orioles
Meet to eat. This gathering's not a flock
but sure is a colorful gathering,
the cardinals, goldfinches, orioles
certainly out-coloring the sparrow
but with a seeming lack of pride in that,
no showing off, each bird having its full
Of what's been provided at the feeder
by me, at considerable expense.
Don't get me wrong. I don't resent at all
this feasting at my feeder all day long
as if by avian entitlement
no slightest bit of gratitude expressed.
There's peeping but not peeped thanks sent my way.
Yet bird colors, bright, subdued are enough
to crown my daylight hours clear on to dusk.
By evening, birds not of a feather
flocked together will be dispersed, depart,
with me worldly wise and left all alone.

DAILY BREAD WITH A VIEW

Able to eat my daily bread in peace
while looking out my window at the trees:
the tall black locust with its tiny leaves,
its pink-white flowers that fall like snowflakes
before the leaves come out, the magnolia,
old as dirt you might say, purple, not pink,
and, off by the stone wall, the cherry tree,
Not yet in bloom but will be very soon,
and then the cherries for my cherry pie
if ravishing blackbirds leave me enough.
Privileged, comfortably housed at peace
munching my daily bread and with a view,
agreeable and more, quite beautiful.
Some years ago I read a troubling line
That would have folks like me called to account,
searing line penned by Archibald MacLeish
from his Depression-era play, *Panic*.
Clearly he meant to reference the Lord's Prayer
which I must say I offer up to God
Our Father, Sunday and every day.
The line begged God forgive our daily bread.

Note: From *Panic* by Archibald MacLeish, cited by Buttrick, "Exposition of Matthew 6:11," in *Interpreter's Bible* 7:313.

A SUBJECT CARESSED

Reading Christopher deVinck this morning
about a quarter to nine with my wife;
thinking through what we read, the subject touched,
you might say caressed, being sex and love,
she and I paused to recall all we could
about their difference and their linkage.

Differentiated in the extreme
loveless sex is lust, unruly desire
getting what it wants, self-satisfaction.
Love is what comes to visit us, to care
for us in our older years—our daughters,
one adopted, two biological,
holding us in their arms and in their prayers,

Just as we hold each other in the night
waiting for the dawn of another day,
as old age would have it: less and less sex
more and more love ". . . long as we both shall live."

Note: DeVinck, *Songs of Innocence and Experience*, 75–76.

Note: Solemnization of Marriage, *The Book of Common Worship* (P.C. U.S.A.) Philadelphia: Board of Christian Education of the General Assembly, 1946, p. 185.

A PRAYER OF LAMENTATION

In response to the Syrian Christian martyrdoms of early 2025.

Ps 133; Matt 5:43–45

My God, where is that ancient heat towards thee,
Wherewith whole shoals of martyrs once did burn,
Besides their other flames?
George Herbert (1593–1633)

Would that the dew of Mount Hermon
would run as tears down the cheeks
of those still living saints of God left
to bewail the coming to grief
and to death of so many of their

Comrade saints whose loss,
grievous and unwarranted,
stains the present life
of those once themselves
cruelly oppressed and slaughtered,

A valiant people whose hope
was to live in peace, secure
despite long frightening years
of tyrannical neglect, worse
terror (poisoned gas death) at the hands

Of a despot whose power
    and whose will to maintain power,
    even now that he is gone,
    staggers the imagination
    of those of us who believe

That we ourselves never could desire
    such a thing as death-dealing
    power akin to his. We've learned
    to cry, How long, O Lord,
    how long shall mercy be delayed,

Forever? Shall love of enemies
    sufficient unto prayers for them
    be left unattempted? Shall hatred,
    lust for getting more than even,
    be our human prospect unendingly?

Shall we become ourselves
    the very thing we hate,
    seize and wield merciless
    power, God forbid, in your name?
    O let tears flow down our cheeks

Like the dew of Mount Hermon.
    And let our prayers be love,
    unceasing prayers of love
    especially for our enemies
    until there are none of them.

LET'S CUP OURSELVES A LIGHTNING BUG

aka Firefly

A little girl, a little boy
Just last night cupped a lightning bug,
Watched its tiny lantern flicker
Off and on, on and off, pure joy.
Perhaps they pondered where's the switch
To flick the lantern off and on,
On and off? Where's the battery?
The little girl showed her delight,
The little boy did too. What awe,
What happy awe they shared last night.
Now you and I, grown up and wise,
Know that it's just biology,
A tiny life form's chemistry.
The childlike wonder in our brains
Is dimmed a bit. It's been this way
For quite some time. Yet there's enough
Of little boy that's left in me,
Enough of little girl in you
To catch at wonder now and then.
Let's cup ourselves a lightning bug
And share once more a child's delight!

THE PRETENDER

John 8:44; 1 Thess 5:1, 2

Ambition's a damnable sprite
That comes like a thief in the night,
An inverted thief so it seems
Filling full your stocking of dreams.
Have you sing like Gordon MacRae,
A fat chance of that any day.
Then tries the accordion scam,
Gets you thinking you're Art Van Damme.
No one else does, but don't you mope,
Ambition resurrects false hope;
Will not leave you languid and bored
But convinced the day of the Lord
Is at hand. Wake up! Wild acclaim's
Yours! You wake up shot down in flames.

NARCISSUS, DAFFODILS, CYNTHIA ROSE

Narcissus, double narcissus
Slender-stemmed with blossoms pure white
Right next to our gold daffodils;
The whole scene is such pure delight
As fills up our backyard with praise.
More praise at our kitchen window,
A single, rare Cynthia rose.
She blooms pink and lovely each year,
Blooms year after year after year!
It is claimed a rose is a rose.
But, heaven knows, this rose we love
Above any rose you can find
Elsewhere. And happily she blooms
July right on till November.
Pink-cheeked, long-lived, dear Cynthia
Cheers our love on, blooming, long-lived.

OUR BEGINNINGS KNOW OUR ENDS

Decades of Christmastide Remembered

At heart I am that little church choir boy
Who's singing in pure boy soprano joy,
On pitch, pure-toned, in cherub choir attire:
Red robe symbolic of that Spirit fire
God lit, a flame of love of God and song,
White bow baptismal sign that I belong
To that great choral host gone on before
Who once on earth, in heaven now, adore
The holy child of Bethlehem, our Lord.
Perhaps you know the hymn; the music soared:

> Once in royal David's city
> Stood a lowly cattle shed,
> Where a mother laid her Baby
> In a manger for His bed:
> Mary was that mother mild,
> Jesus Christ, her little Child.
>
> He came down to earth from heaven
> Who is God and Lord of all,
> And His shelter was a stable,
> And His cradle was a stall:
> With the poor, and mean, and lowly,
> Lived on earth our Savior holy.

Jesus is our childhoods' pattern,
Day by day like us he grew;
He was little, weak, and helpless,
Tears and smiles like us He knew:
And He feeleth for our sadness,
And He shareth in our gladness.

And our eyes at last shall see Him,
Through His own redeeming love;
For that child so dear and gentle
Is our Lord in heaven above,
And he leads His children on
To the place where He is gone.

Note: "Once in Royal David's City," Cecil Frances Alexander (1848), in Jones, *Hymnbook*, hymn no. 462. Ms. Alexander wrote an entire volume of cherished children's hymnody.

AFTER ALL

Some Thoughts on Iconography

The subject is vast and I certainly am more grasped by it than it by me. Long years ago a friend of mine took exception to my thoughts on a matter of moral discernment being vigorously debated in the churches. He wrote to me: "Chuck, you're in over your head." Perhaps I was then. No doubt I am now. But, since I always found it easier to swim underwater than on the surface I will proceed.

My plunge into iconography is not to be taken as a searching out of iconographic meaning as understood in Eastern Orthodoxy. For devout believers in that ecclesial tradition icons are indispensable to faith and to what it means to be held in the communion of saints. Sculpture, painting, statuary also are of utmost importance in the Roman Catholic tradition. In the Protestant traditions (especially my tradition, the Reformed tradition) there is considerable hesitance with regard to the use of visual imagery in worship and even in the personal piety of believers. But it is not banished entirely, and, among some believers, pictorial depictions of biblical events and persons have pedagogical importance. I am not using the term iconography in the popular and media sense either. John Lewis rightly is considered a civil rights icon. He is deceased, but his contribution to the civil rights movement is unfading. He is remembered, made present with the ongoing struggle to ensure civil rights for all. In the same sense Katharine Hepburn is an icon of the silver screen. Langston Hughes has iconic status as a poet.

My use of the term iconography does have something in common with both traditional religious understandings of the term and its popular use in our culture. Iconography suggests felt presence, the presence of the saints in the communion of saints, the presence (or meaningful memory of) persons whose influence upon movements in the public realm and in the arts is unforgettable, singularly important, generation after generation.

I believe that the Holy Scriptures of the Judeo-Christian tradition can be thought of as verbal iconography. With them God makes his presence felt in judgment and mercy, claim and succor, the two sides of the single coin of God's grace. Just so the Scriptures may be considered a means of grace, *the* means of grace. It has been put this way: the Bible gives us a place to stand to hear God speak to us today. Are we listening? If we are listening we need to pray for the illumination of the Holy Spirit to guide our hearing as we roam the world of the Bible.

Theologians have pointed out that we are bound to the appointed means of grace: word, sacrament, and prayer. But God is not so bound. There are the so-called extraordinary means of grace by which he may choose to make himself known. Above all God may make Godself known in the created order, the things that he has made. The Bible speaks of God's making his "power and divine nature" (Rom 1:20) known there. Using a nineteenth-century phrase that I find still appealing, the presence of God may be read and felt in *The Book of Nature*.

Now after all is said and done I remain in over my head when it comes to these matters of iconography, grace, the mystery of God's self-disclosure in Jesus Christ, the witness of Holy Scripture to him, and his revelation of himself—his felt presence in—*The Book of Nature*. But again, after all, *deus cognitus, deus nullus*: God comprehended is no God and the religion or theology or piety that pretends otherwise is a sham. We know God is love but we do not comprehend God. And the love of God is itself a vast mystery getting hold of us. I suspect that to think otherwise is to never have known it, felt the unyielding grip of it. Yet, to quote Robert Browning,

. . . Christ rises! Mercy every way
Is infinite,—and who can say?

Note: Robert Browning, "Christmas Eve and Easter Day," stanza 33, in *Browning's Complete Poetical Works*, ed. Horaca E. Scudder (Boston: Houghton Mifflin, 1895), p. 335.

Off the Bookshelf

A brief list of references especially informing the approach taken in the preceding pages to poetic form, Scripture, verbal iconography, and notions of presences and Real Presence.

Adams, Marilyn McCord. *Horrendous Evils and the Goodness of God*. Ithaca, NY: Cornell University Press, 1999.

Alighieri, Dante. *The Divine Comedy*. Translated by Henry F. Cary. New York: P. F. Collier & Sons, 1937.

Ammons, A. R. "Corson's Inlet." In *Collected Poems 1951–1971*, 147–51. New York: Norton, 1972.

Augustine. *The Confessions of Saint Augustine*. Translated by Edward B. Pusy. London: Collier-Macmillan, 1961.

Ballie, John. *The Sense of the Presence of God*. New York: Charles Scribner's Sons, 1962.

Barth, Karl. *The Humanity of God*. Richmond, VA: John Knox, 1960.

Berleant, Arnold. *Art and Engagement*. Philadelphia: Temple University Press, 1991.

Bishop, Elizabeth. *The Complete Poems 1927–1979*. New York: Farrar, Straus and Giroux, 1983.

Black, C. Clifton. *Mark's Gospel: History, Theology, Interpretation*. Grand Rapids: Eerdmans, 2023.

Bloom, Harold. *The Best Poems of the English Language: From Chaucer Through Robert Frost*. New York: Harper Perennial, 2004.

Bontemps, Arna, ed. *American Negro Poetry*. New York: Hill and Wang, 1963.

Brown, Frank Burch. *Religious Aesthetics: A Theological Study of Making and Meaning*. Princeton, NJ: Princeton University Press, 1989.

Browning, Elizabeth Barrett. *The Complete Works of Elizabeth Barrett Browning*, edited by Horace E. Scudder, 191. New York: Houghton Mifflin, 1900.

Browning, Robert. *The Complete Poetic and Dramatic Works of Robert Browning*. Edited by Horace E. Scudder. New York: Houghton Mifflin, 1895.

Brueggemann, Walter. *Finally Comes the Poet: Daring Speech for Proclamation.* Minneapolis: Fortress, 1989.

Calvin, John. *Institutes of the Christian Religion* 1–2. Edited by John T. McNeill. Translated by Ford Lewis Battles. Philadelphia: Westminster, 1960.

DeVinck, Christopher, *Songs of Innocence and Experience.* New York: Viking, 1994.

Dyrness, William A. *Senses of the Soul: Art and the Visual in Christian Worship.* Eugene, OR: Cascade, 2008.

Emerson, Ralph Waldo. *Essays and English Traits.* Edited by Charles W. Eliot. New York: P. F. Collier & Sons, 1937.

Farmer, H. H. *The Servant of the Word.* Philadelphia: Fortress, 1964.

Farrer, Austin. *The Glass of Vision.* Westminster: Dacre, 1948.

Frost, Robert. "Pertinax." In *The Poetry of Robert Frost*, edited by Edward Connery Latham, 308. New York: Holt, Rinehart and Winston, 1969.

Glory to God: The Presbyterian Hymnal. Louisville, KY: Westminster John Knox Press, 2013.

Green, Garrett. *Imagining God: Theology and the Religious Imagination.* San Francisco: Harper and Row, 1989.

Guite, Malcolm. *Faith, Hope and Poetry: Theology and the Poetic Imagination.* Burlington, VT: Ashgate, 2010.

———. "Something Holy Shines." *Christianity Today* 59 (2025) 70–77.

Hart, David Bentley. *The Beauty of the Infinite: The Aesthetics of Christian Truth.* Grand Rapids: Eerdmans, 2003.

Hass, Robert. *A Little Book on Form: An Exploration into the Formal Imagination of Poetry.* San Francisco: Harper Collins, 2017.

Jones, David Hugh. *The Hymnbook.* Philadelphia: John Ribble, 1955.

Langer, Susanne K. *Feeling and Form: A Theology of Art Developed from Philosophy in a New Key.* New York: Charles Scribner's Sons, 1953.

Lares, Jameela. *Milton and the Preaching Arts.* Pittsburgh: Duquesne University Press, 2001.

Le Guin, Ursula K. *So Far So Good: Final Poems 2014–2018.* Port Townsend, WA: Copper Canyon, 2018.

Lockerbie, D. Bruce. *The Timeless Moment: Creativity and the Christian Faith.* Westchester, IL: Cornerstone, 1980.

Long, Thomas G. *Preaching and the Literary Forms of the Bible.* Philadelphia: Fortress, 1989.

Metzger, Bruce M., and Roland E. Murphy, eds. *The New Oxford Annotated Bible with the Apocryphal/Deuterocanonical Books.* New York: Oxford University Press, 1996.

Milliner, Matthew J. *The Everlasting People: G. K. Chesterton and the First Nations.* Downers Grove, IL: InterVarsity, 2021.

———. *Mother of the Lamb: The Story of a Global Icon.* Minneapolis, MN: Fortress, 2022.

Neal, Jerusha Matson. *Holy Ground: Climate Change, Preaching, and the Apocalypse of Place.* Waco, TX: Baylor University Press, 2024.

Newmann, Eric. *The Origins and History of Consciousness*. Princeton, NJ: Princeton University Press, 2014.

Parker, DeWitt H. *The Principles of Aesthetics*. 2nd ed. New York: Appleton-Century-Crofts, 1946.

Rader, Melvin. *A Modern Book of Esthetics: An Anthology*. New York: Henry Holt and Company, 1952.

Santayana, George. "O World." In *A Concise Treasury of Great Poems, English and American*, edited by Louis Untermeyer, 397. New York: Simon & Schuster, 1942.

Shakespeare, William. *The Tragedy of Hamlet, Prince of Denmark*. Edited by Edward Hubler. New York: The New American Library, 1963.

Steiner, George. *Real Presences*. London: Faber and Faber, 1989.

Strawn, Brent A. *The Incomparable God: Readings in Biblical Theology*. Edited by Collin Cornell and M. Justin Walker. Grand Rapids: Eerdmans, 2023.

Terrien, Samuel. *Job: Poet of Existence*. New York: Bobbs-Merrill, 1957.

———. *The Psalms: Strophic Structure and Theological Commentary*. Grand Rapids: Eerdmans, 2003.

Tillich, Paul. *Systematic Theology* 1. Chicago: The University of Chicago Press, 1951.

Torrance, Andrew. "The Crux of Creation." *Christianity Today* 59 (2025) 46–49.

Wilder, Amos N. *Modern Poetry and the Christian Tradition: A Study in the Relation of Christianity to Culture*. New York: Charles Scribner's Sons, 1952.

Wordsworth, William. "The World Is Too Much with Us." In *Romantic Poets: Blake to Poe*, edited by W. H. Auden and Norman Holmes Pearson, 168. New York: Viking, 1950.

www.ingramcontent.com/pod-product-compliance
Lightning Source LLC
LaVergne TN
LVHW050537100826
845148LV00002B/589

* 9 7 9 8 3 8 5 2 6 4 6 7 4 *